The Bespoke O⋁

A Play

Wolf Mankowitz

Samuel French – London
New York – Sydney – Toronto – Hollywood

CHARACTERS

Morry, a tailor
Fender, a warehouse clerk
Ranting, his employer
A Clerk

AUTHOR'S NOTE

Love is a luxury which very poor people can afford, and *The Bespoke Overcoat* is a story of this love. It is not a love which conquers all. Fender does not get enough food, or a tailor-made overcoat, in this life. In life he does not find satisfaction, except in so far as he is able to accept with humour and humility the deprivations forced upon him. It is because this humour and humility is shared with his friend that Fender, in spite of everything, would prefer to go on living. To prefer to go on living is to love in the context of this story and, because this is loving at its most deprived, the story is a sad one.

In producing *The Bespoke Overcoat* that remarkable artist Alec Clunes concentrated entirely upon this feeling which, by its intensity, animates a piece which is not well-constructed. The story was written without any direction for staging or the production of effects. The only stage, the only effects, the only theatre I had in mind were in the heart of a drunken tailor. There was no indication of time past or time present, because a twinge of conscience lasts a moment or a life-time, and *The Bespoke Overcoat* is about the unreasonable conscience felt by the poor who love the poorer with a love which conquers nothing.

So Alec Clunes' production, which was, in effect, the writing of the play for the practical stage, dispensed with sets, used the barest properties, used darkness broken by three constantly moving areas of light, to tell a simple story with great simplicity. He realized that Fender was not a ghost and that this story was not a ghost-story; he understood that *The Bespoke Overcoat* was a sustained, typically over-long Jewish joke—than which there is no sadder and no funnier story. And I am deeply grateful to him for having understood so much, for having made it available to other people, and for having taught me in the process, as he has taught so many other artists, something of the meaning of theatre.

WOLF MANKOWITZ

THE BESPOKE OVERCOAT

SCENE I

The action of the play is distributed among three separate areas permanently set and used in turn.

Area "A", midstage R., is RANTING'S *warehouse, which consists of a sizeable table, placed obliquely, with a chair or stool L. and to the U.S. end of it. U.S. of the table, and rather behind it, a large rack supports a selection of overcoats on hangers.*

Area "B" is D.S.C. and has no furnishing.

Area "C", midstage L., is MORRY'S *room, which consists of a mattress lying obliquely on the floor, and beside it R., at the U.S. end, a chair.*

These three areas are encompassed by a black surround with entrances D.R., D.L., and U.C. During the entire play, these are in total darkness, as are any two of the acting areas not being used. Throughout, the stage directions will be related to the areas described.

When the curtain rises MORRY *is standing in the area "B", with a navy blue overcoat over his arm. A barrel organ is playing, off, and fades out as the light at "B" fades in.*

MORRY. Fender dead. That old man Fender dead. Funny thing. You're a good tailor, he used to say. You're a good tailor. No, you're a good tailor. Look around. I don't care where you look, he says, you are a number one tailor. Look at this coat, he says. What, that old coat? A coat must be twenty years old. Mind you, I can tell straightaway by the cross-stitch it's my coat. It's your coat, he shouts. You made it. Twenty-two years ago I come to you for a coat. This is him. I still got him. You got a good point. I tell him, I'm a good tailor. It's only the truth. I'm a good tailor. Straightaway, I see I made a mistake. I fell in. How much, Fender says, will you take to mend a coat like this? I ask you. It's falling to pieces on his back. I told him straight, no nonsense. Look, Fender, I told him, I can run you up a pair of trousers from lining canvas you can walk up Saville Road nobody can tell you from the Prince of Wales. But, Fender, do me a favour. Take the coat somewhere else. A new coat I can make, but the Union says no miracles. A rag, that's all. I got my clients to think about. Good afternoon. A lovely piece of worsted. Mind you, I got a suit length here: in a hundred year you wouldn't see nothing better. Clients. Fender dead. An old man. (*Turns U.S., still speaking.*) He sits in that stone cold warehouse all day long. (*Turns head round to audience.*) Who could mend such a coat? (*Moves slowly* U.S. *to* C. *exit.*) That's enough. (*Light starts to fade.*) Leave me alone. All this nagging, nagging. (*He has gone, and so has the light.*)

SCENE 2

*As the light fades in on "*C*". sitting cross-legged and hunched on* MORRY'S *mattress is* FENDER. *He rubs his hands.*

FENDER. Oi. How that Morry can thread a needle in this cold, I don't know. Such a cold.

MORRY (*entering* U.S.C.). I got trouble of my own. After all, I'm in Bond Street? I'm a merchant prince? I'm not even a limited company.

FENDER. I thought you was a limited company.

MORRY (*turning*). Me? Never. What do I want with shares and directors? So—what can I do for you? It's late, but . . .

FENDER. To be managing director is not a nice thing? You got no ambition? Terrible cold in here. My old guvernor—managing director three companies. Chairman—six companies. But what a man! (*Rises.*) Look, Morry. I still got no overcoat. Put on the gas ring.

MORRY. Fender! You ain't dead?

FENDER. Sure I'm dead. Would I sit up half the night in the freezing cold if I wasn't dead? I can tell you, I won't be sorry to get back. They got central heating, constant hot water, room service. And the food—as much as you like. Kosher, of course.

MORRY (*holding his head*). I won't touch the rotten brandy.

FENDER. Drinks? You can have what you like, any time, day or night, on the house.

MORRY. Go on. So tell me, Fender. Is it really you?

FENDER (*holding out his hand*). Feel my hand. Feel.

MORRY (*taking his hand*). Believe me, you are cold. That lousy brandy. It kills you. (*Sneezes.*)

FENDER (*sitting on chair*). Gesundheit.

MORRY. Thank you.

FENDER. All I want is to get back. Listen, Morry. You know the first person I met down there?

MORRY. Down there?

FENDER. I tell you, Morry, a secret: everybody goes down there. You know who I met? Lennie.

MORRY. Lennie from Fournier Street?

FENDER. Who else? He's doing the same job. And *what* herrings! I tell you, Morry, I won't be sorry to get back.

MORRY (*kneeling on mattress*). Fender! You don't hold that overcoat against me, do you Fender? Believe me, if I had known you would catched a cold and died I would give you my own coat.

FENDER. That blankety coat. For that coat I'm here and not at the hotel. Look, Morry. I got nothing against you.

MORRY (*rising to one knee*). You ain't going to haunt me, Fender? You wouldn't haunt an old friend?

FENDER. Don't talk silly, Morry. That haunting is a special job. They don't give it to new residents. For haunting you get a commission.

MORRY (*rising and moving behind* FENDER. *Crossing arms*). So listen, Fender. It goes without saying I am pleased to see you. I'm glad you enjoy being dead. But you won't think I am rude, if I ask what you want of my life?

FENDER. I'll tell you. But first light that gas-ring so at least I won't freeze—listen to me—to death, I nearly said. You don't know, Morry, (*The light begins to fade.*) what sort of life it was at that Ranting clothing company. No wonder I didn't lose any sleep about dying . . . (*The light has gone.*)

SCENE 3

The light fades in on "A". FENDER *is sitting on the stool with his notebook and pencil on the table in front of him. The conversation continues from the previous* SCENE.

FENDER. After that warehouse for forty-three years, any change would be a pleasure. Forty-three years a shipping clerk.

MORRY (*off*). So long?

FENDER. Forty-three years next Purim, if I didn't die before.

(RANTING *enters* D.R. *carrying a board with lists.*)

RANTING (*to behind desk*). And sixty gross denim trousers.

FENDER (*writing*). Sixty gross denim trousers.

RANTING. And forty gross cellaloid collars.

FENDER. Cellaloid collars. Forty gross cellaloid.

RANTING (*tapping with pencil, impatiently*). Cellaloid makes with a C, no S.

FENDER. And what more?

RANTING. Eleven dozen raincoats, Prussian collar.

FENDER. Eleven dozen raincoats.

RANTING. Prussian collar.

FENDER. You know something, Mr. Ranting? It's cold in this warehouse. I said it's cold, Mr. Ranting. I feel the cold something terrible.

RANTING. Fender, I don't think you enjoy your work like in the olden days. (*Sits on table, head turned half* D.S. *towards* FENDER.)

FENDER. What an idea! I enjoy my work? Certainly I enjoy. I feel the cold, that's all.

RANTING. Naturally, you are getting on. The work is hard. Nobody is as young as he used to be.

FENDER. What are you talking, Mr. Ranting? Nobody is as young as he used to be? And how could he?

RANTING. I am saying, Fender, an old man is an old man.

FENDER (*rises*). Certainly. Of course. An old man is an old man. Mr. Ranting, I tell you something: my father, when he was seventy—no, over seventy—he can bend a horseshoe straight with his bare hands. And even he felt the cold.

RANTING (*getting off table*). All I am saying, Fender, is stop driving me mad with your crying "it's so cold, it's so cold". Get a new overcoat; you won't feel it.

FENDER. I make an arrangement with you, Mr. Ranting. I'll take one of the overcoats, the big ones with the sheep-skin lining, and every week from my wages take off a certain sum. (*Holds out his hands.*) A proposition, Mr. Ranting?

RANTING. One of them coats, Fender? Leave me alone. (FENDER *moves as if to speak.*) Hup! A coat like this is worth twenty pound anybody's money. What do you make? With all due respect, Fender, what do you make? You won't live so long to pay off such a coat.

FENDER (*sitting on stool, again*). That's true. So what can you do?

RANTING (*reading from list*). Seventeen dozen pair shooting breeches.

FENDER (*writing*). Seventeen dozen pair breeches.

RANTING. Shooting.

FENDER. Shooting, shooting. (*Indicates the entry in his book.*)

RANTING (*in disgust*). Ah! (*Exit* D.R.)

FENDER (*rising and taking off his coat*). Maybe Morry can mend the old coat again. (*Cross fade lights from "A" to "C".*) After all he's a good tailor. (*Turns* U.S. *as the light goes.*)

SCENE 4

(*As the light fades in on "C"* FENDER *is standing* U.S. *of mattress.* MORRY *enters* D.L.)

MORRY. Look, Fender, look. The seams is all rotten. Look, the lining is like ribbons. Look, the material is threadbare.

FENDER. A tailor like you, Morry, to make such a fuss. You should be ashamed.

MORRY (*sitting on chair*). The padding is like an old horse blanket.

FENDER. Who asks for new padding? Only make the coat good. Who cares about the padding, so long as the coat is warm?

MORRY. It can't be done.

FENDER. Don't make jokes, Morry.

MORRY. If I say it can't be done, it can't be done.

FENDER. So, all right, charge a little more.

MORRY. Charge! What does charge matter? It can't be done.

FENDER. Why are you so hard for, Morry? After all, you can patch with off cuts. (MORRY *holds head in hands.*) I am not asking, after all, for West End style; I should look so smart. I don't care how smart. Only mend the coat, Morry.

MORRY. Fender, listen to me, Fender. A good coat like I make has got twenty years wear. I double stitch the seams with best thread, no rubbish. Every stitch I test, (*Bites imaginary thread.*) so it's good and strong. I use good material: crombie, tweed, what you like. The best. I use a lovely lining; someone else would make a wedding dress from it, such a lining I use.

FENDER. You use marvellous lining, Morry.

MORRY. I make the whole coat, the buttons holes, the pockets, every-thing.

FENDER. Don't I tell everybody? Morry—a needle like Paganini. I tell everybody.

MORRY. I would make you such a coat for cost, Fender.

FENDER. How much costs such a coat?

MORRY. Three yards, say.

FENDER. Say two and a half.

MORRY. And lining.

FENDER. Don't worry yourself with lining.

MORRY. I can make you a good coat for twelve pound.

FENDER. You can't mend the old coat?

MORRY. Please, Fender, do me a favour.

FENDER. I can ask? Twelve pound if money.

MORRY (*rises*). Listen, Fender. I break my neck: ten pound for the coat. You got ten pound?

FENDER. I look like a banker? I can save ten pound.

MORRY. So.

FENDER (*as he starts to put on his old coat*). So. So I'm going to have made a bespoke overcoat.

MORRY. Bespoke is good.

FENDER. Certainly bespoke. You think I would wear Ranting's rubbish? (*Sits on chair.*)

MORRY (*moving* D.S.L. *and reaching off-stage for patterns*). What material you like?

FENDER. I can choose materials?

MORRY (*to* FENDER *with patterns*). Here, patterns.

FENDER. The grey is not nice for me. The blue is better?

MORRY (*fingering the blue material*). Blue is nice. You can wear blue for any occasion.

FENDER. Nigger brown is smart.

MORRY. For a young man.

FENDER. Black is always good.

MORRY. Black is good, but a nice, dark blue is nicer.
FENDER (*rising, and moving* D.S. *of mattress*). Believe me, Morry, I think
you are right. The blue is good—and thick. What a material!
MORRY (*down to* FENDER). I should say. So you can save ten pounds?
FENDER. Save? Sure I can save. And old man like me, if I got an
overcoat, what do I need? (*Moving* D.S.C. *to* "B".) If I got a bespoke
overcoat, what more can I need? (*Exit into darkness* D.R.)

SCENE 5

MORRY *takes out black bread etc. from his pocket and moves to
his chair.*
MORRY. With a piece of black bread and a herring you can't go wrong.
You got in black bread vitamins, nutriment *and* a good flavour from
herrings. In the old days, (*Sits.*) sometimes six clients a week, all
wanting coats, suits, a spare pair of trousers, something. The trade
is not good any more. Believe me, if I had a boy I wouldn't let
him see a needle and thread. It's a thing of the past. Things are so
bad now, you know what I'm doing? I'm making a ten pound coat
for Fender. For ten pounds, it's a wonderful coat. The material,
the seams. No wind can blow through a coat like this. (*Rises and
moves* D.S. *a few paces.*) Let it blow as much as it likes. I read an
interesting thing somewhere. When it's cold, it's not really cold.
You are hot; that's why you feel the cold. Also you pull in your
muscles. That's bad. Fender: his trouble is he's pulled his muscles
so far in they won't pull any more. (*Moving* D.L. *to exit, as light
fades.*) I was always interested in science things like this. (*Cross
fade to* "B".)

SCENE 6

RANTING *enters* D.R. *with a plate of chopped liver and a fork.*
RANTING. The chopped liver is tukke good, Alf. You want some?
Good boy. (*Stops* D.C. "B".) Bring some more chopped liver, Maisie.
So I was telling you, Alf: this exhibition they got such machines
you wouldn't believe. They got a machine there, (I'm not tell you
a word of a lie, Alf) they got a machine can add up how much you
made last year, take away your overheads, knock off your income
tax, and show you if you got anything left. By my life. It has a
dictation machine, a suspended filing system, a place special for
telephone directories, and a permutator for working out football
pools so they should win. And I worry myself to nothing, worrying, worrying the whole time over an old clerk's mistakes. What
you say? Can a machine laugh like a man? Can it cry like a man?
What difference? So long as a clerk clerks good, what difference he's
laughing or crying? (*Exit* D.R. *in blackout as we hear* FENDER *laugh, off.*)

SCENE 7

The light fades in on FENDER, *laughing quietly, as he enters* D.R. *and moves to "*A*" below table, with the baigel half eaten and wrapped in paper.*

FENDER. A marvellous story, I must tell it to Moiry. I enjoy a good laugh. (*He sighs and looks at the baigel.*) A baigel is enough. After all, bread and salt is food. It's the same dinner, only I leave out the soup. That woman, terrible, but what soup. I'm not saying it's not worth a sixpence. A bowl like that, where could you get it for sixpence? In a big restaurant they bring you half as much, and charge terrible prices. A woman cooks soup like that must make somebody a marvellous wife. Mind you, boss-eyed and what temper, a terrible woman. Still a baigel is plenty. Eat it slow, careful, every crumb does you good. Soup! who wants soup? (*Moves* U.S.) When I get the coat, I put it on. I walk up to a table, (*Sits.*) I sit down in the overcoat, blue, nice: a bowl of soup, missus, and a baigel. (*Rises and moves a few paces* D.S.) Be careful! You want the soup should drop on this new overcoat—a bespoke overcoat—ruined. (*He laughs as, lifting the flap of his torn coat, his hand slips through a hole.*) I don't think I got room for these bits. No, I'm full up. I couldn't eat another thing, not even a fresh lutka or a piece of cheesecake. (*Turns to his accounts.*) Sixteen dozen flying jackets. (U.S. *to sit.*) With such jackets you can fly?

RANTING (*enters* D.R., *moves behind table from which he brushes crumbs*). How many times, Fender? Don't eat in the warehouse. It brings the mice. The mice eat the clothing.

FENDER. How many clothing can a little mouse eat?

RANTING (*reading*). Twenty-eight gross denim trousers. (*Fade out.*)

SCENE 8

*Area "*C*". Fade in on* FENDER *entering breathlessly* U.C.

FENDER (*calls*). Morry, I come to see how the coat is coming, Morry.

MORRY (*footsteps, off*). The coat is all right.

FENDER. Which is the coat, Morry?

MORRY (*entering* D.L., *with half-made coat*). Here! Here!

FENDER. Should I try it on?

MORRY (*holding out coat*). Try it on. Don't be shy. What's a matter with you? You're a film starlet, you got to have a changing room else you can't take off the old coat. (FENDER *removes coat*.) So. That's right. Take it off.

(FENDER *gives his coat to* MORRY, *who puts it on chair, and puts on the new coat*.)

FENDER. If I knew, I would put my other shirt on. You seen it, Morry? The drill shirt, with tabs on the shoulders, very smart.

MORRY. And why should you? Today is a bank holiday? Look. My own shirt. Everybody wears his old shirt for a working day. Nu. Try it.

FENDER (*as* MORRY *fits the coat*). In Clacton the sun is hot. This makes him the sun, you understand. What a hot! You got a nice deck chair, Mrs. Felderman. I can see. A comfortable deck chair. Certainly a new overcoat—a bespoke overcoat. (*Lifts the left arm with sleeve in it.*) Suits me? Under the arms is a bit tight.

MORRY (*feeling armhole*). It's fine. You got plenty room, look, look.

FENDER. A coat like this makes a difference.

MORRY (*kneeling in front to fit coat*). Fender, you like the coat? What about a couple of pound on account? I got expenses. (*Rising.*) Can you manage a couple?

> (FENDER *takes out purse, sorts out notes and silver, and hands them over with great dignity.*)

FENDER. Certainly. You know, Morry, twenty shillings, if you saved money like I do, thirty shillings, and didn't throw it away on that rotten brandy, thirty-five shillings, you would be a rich man. Forty shillings.

MORRY. And what would I do with my money?

FENDER. A question. What can you do with it?

MORRY. I can take an off-licence.

FENDER. An off-licence is a good idea. (*Taking off new coat.*)

MORRY. I use my knowledge. A special line in brandy. Old stuff—Napoleon—something good. (*Takes overcoat from* FENDER *and hands him his old one.*)

FENDER. How can you know it's good?

MORRY. I try every bottle, personal. I put up a smart notice, Morry's Napoleon Brandy; every bottle personal tasted. Thanks for the two pound. You can spare?

FENDER. Sure I can spare. The coat won't be long now, Morry?

MORRY. This week I make an exception. I have a drink tonight; that way tomorrow I take less.

FENDER. Tukke?

MORRY. Listen, Fender, drinking is by me not by you; it's my hobby so I shouldn't know? (*Exeunt. Cross fade to* "B".)

SCENE 9

When the lights go up on "B", RANTING *is straphanging* D.S.C.

RANTING (*in a new coat*). On the Central Line is always hot. You like the coat? Yesterday I picked it up. America style. (*Lurches.*) Sorry, miss. Dear? I should say it's dear! You want me to wear one of me own coats? Twenty-five nicker—a pony, this coat—I beg your pardon. Knock off the booze and you'll be able to afford. My advice to you friend, is—knock off the demon drink.

He goes out D.R. *Cross fade to* "C".

SCENE 10

FENDER *is asleep on* MORRY'S *mattress, covered by the half-finished overcoat.* MORRY *enters drunkenly,* U.S.C., *singing and carrying a bottle.*

MORRY. It says on the label extra special reserve, cognac Napoleon brandy, old special reserve. A brandy like this is a brandy like this. This. (*Drinks.*) A brandy. (*Turns to mattress.*) I got company? So late? (U.S. *to put bottle on chair.*) Hey, wake up. I got company. You sit here a minute. Don't go way. I'll come back. (*Kneeling* U.S. *of mattress.*) Wake up, Fender, it's you? What an unexpected pleasure.

FENDER (*sitting up*). I was having a dream. A flying overcoat and inside the pockets bowls of soup. And do you know, the soup never upset in the coat.

MORRY. I got here a brandy; you never drunk such a brandy in your life.

FENDER (*peering at the label*). Special reserve. Must be good.

MORRY. Take a little drop. Go on. Take.

FENDER (*trying it*). Ahh, like fire. (*Hands bottle back.*) A good one all right. Morry—Moishele.

MORRY (*holding out bottle in front of him*). It's good brandy.

FENDER. I got bad news, Morry.

MORRY. Where can you find a brandy like this?

FENDER. That Ranting. He give me the sack.

MORRY (*as he sits back on his heels and puts bottle on floor with a thud*). He give you the sack?

FENDER. He give me the sack.

MORRY. After so long he give you the sack?

FENDER. He give me.

MORRY. He give it to *you?*

FENDER. The sack.

MORRY. Oi.

FENDER. I have with great regrets, Morry I must tell you, to cancel the coat. I came to tell you. Cancel the coat.

MORRY (*trying to give him the bottle*). Take another drop brandy. Good for your cough.

FENDER. I don't fancy.

MORRY. Take. Don't be shy. (FENDER *drinks from bottle, and as he lifts his arm we see that the old coat is torn under the arm.*) If I could mend

that coat, Fender, I would mend it, I want you to know. I defy
any master tailor to make that coat good.
FENDER. What can you do? It's just an old coat, that's all.
MORRY (*rises*). You can't find the rest of the ten pounds? I'll finish
the coat.
FENDER. How?
MORRY (*puts arm round* FENDER *and pats him on shoulder*). With a
needle. How else?

The lights slowly fade.

SCENE 11

FENDER (*at* "B", D.S.C.). I told him, polite, but strong. Mr. Ranting,
I been with this firm with your father and your uncle so many
years. All this time I done the same job; nobody complains. Sud-
denly business is so bad you have to turn me off? Let him answer
that. No good. Excuses, anybody can find excuses. What I ask
you, Mr. Ranting, is, is it right? Let him answer me that. That's
what I should have said. I should have told him off, big as he is.
The governor, (*Turns* U.S. *and spits.*) I used to give him a handker-
chief he should wipe his nose. A little boy crying round the warehouse with his stockings down gives me the sack. Why didn't I tell
him? Fender, he says, you got something put by, an insurance
policy, something? I got something put by, don't worry. You got
no family? Don't worry, I got plenty of family, I got friends. He
worries about me. I even got a niece with a boarding-house in
Clacton, and can she cook? Lovely weather the whole time. (*Turns*
U.S.C. *and then back to audience.*) Mind you, Morry is a good friend.
In the morning I put on my new coat. I go to Ranting. I tell him.
Give me that coat with the sheepskin. (*Coughs.*) Funny thing, a
cough like this, comes right through you. Like a bowl of soup. It
flies up through you like a flying jacket. There he goes. (*He traces the
path of the imaginary jacket round the theatre. It returns as the threatening
celluloid collars.* FENDER *is dying.*) Seventeen dozen celluloid collars,
celluloid makes with a C, not S—or S, no C. (*Weakly.*) Funny
thing, I don't seem to know nothing any more. (*Sinks down as the
lights slowly fade.*)

SCENE 12

The lights fade in on area "A" *as a* CLERK, *followed by* RANTING,
enters D.R. RANTING *goes* U.S. *to behind table.* CLERK *sits at table with
notebook and pencil.*
RANTING. Thirty dozen pair shooting breeches.
CLERK. Thirty dozen pair shooting breeches.
RANTING. And a hundred dozen Balaclava helmets.

(MORRY *enters* U.S.C. *with finished overcoat over his arm.*)
MORRY (*coming to* U.S. *of table*). Mr. Ranting. Excuse me, Mr. Ranting.
RANTING. And sixty various drill jackets. Can I help you, sir?
MORRY. I come for Fender. I finished him a coat.
RANTING. And two gross khaki drill shorts. He don't work here no
     more. I say work, but you should understand he was past it.
CLERK. Two gross shorts.
RANTING. Khaki drill.
CLERK. What?
MORRY. Khaki drill.
RANTING. Thank you. Fender lives by the arches in Flower and Dean
     Street. Or maybe with his niece at Clacton or somewhere. Pardon
     me. And twenty-eight pith helmets. (*Exit* D.S.R.) Ah!
CLERK. Twenty-eight pith helmets. (*Rests his arms and head on table.*)
                    Cross fade "A" *to* "C".

SCENE 13

Area "C", *continuing as from* SCENE 2; MORRY *is* U.S. *of mattress,*
     level with FENDER, *who sits in chair.*
MORRY. So I go to your lodging. I knock on the door. No answer.
     I knock again. An old woman comes. She's a bit deaf.
FENDER. She's stone deaf. A bit, he says.
MORRY. I shout in her ear, where is Fender? Fender—Fender! where
     should he be? He's dead. He didn't have my age, but he's dead.
     You can knock me over with a feather bed.
FENDER. She got her head screwed on, the old girl. I was dead all
     right. Mind you, she makes out she's older than she is. I don't like
     that sort of thing.
MORRY. But so sudden.
FENDER (*rising and crossing in front of* MORRY). Listen, Morry. You die
     when you are ready? You die when you have to, that's all. Still, I
     haven't done so bad. I can't complain. If only I kept my mouth
     shut I would be all right.
MORRY. I made the coat as quick as I can, Fender. (*Sits in chair.*)
FENDER. Look, Morry, I got nothing against you. You behave like
     a perfect gentleman. I told everybody at the hotel. Morry's a
     wonderful tailor. You think you look smart? Wait until Morry
     gets here. No. It was that Ranting. You see, Morry, I didn't take
     too long dying, but the whilst I am screaming and cursing, using
     terrible language, all against that Ranting. And when I get down
     there, it must have been on my mind. So the first couple of weeks,
     I am stopping the porter, the commissionaire, the chamber-maids,
     even the guests, telling them about the overcoat. At last, they can't
     stand it any more. The manager sends for me. Fender, he says,

you like the hotel? It's a wonderful hotel, I tell him. Everything of the best. I am very satisfied. Look, Fender, he says, I am very glad if you are comfortable, but I have to tell you everyone has a headache with your overcoat. Do me a favour: go down to the cloakroom, pick yourself any coat. Thank you, I tell him. It's not the same. I can see he is upset. I can't have the place turned upside down, he says. (*Pointing upwards.*) You'll have to go back for a while. When you get it, (*Points downwards.*) come back. It's on my mind, I told him. Next thing I know, I'm here. And here I am.

MORRY (*half rises*). And I got your overcoat all wrapped up ready, Fender. Take it and good luck to you.

FENDER (*moving D.s. level with bottom of mattress*). It's no good, Morry. It wouldn't make me happy. Somehow, I got to have that sheepskin coat from Ranting. I am not saying your coat isn't wonderful. It is. But I must have from Ranting a coat. I give him forty-three years nearly. He must give me a coat.

MORRY (*moving down to* FENDER *with bottle*). You know what?

FENDER. What?

MORRY. We go to Rantings and take the coat. That's what. (*Drinks.*)

FENDER (*as* MORRY *offers him the bottle*). Not a bad idea. (*Drinks and returns bottle. Exeunt D.S.L. with* MORRY'S *arm round* FENDER. *Cross fade to* "A".)

SCENE 14

As the light fades in on "A", RANTING *enters from* U.S.C., *singing. The* CLERK *is seated at the table, writing in his notebook.*

RANTING. That book you been making up for the past hour, what's the matter, you can't read?

CLERK. The old clerk had his own way of doing things. It takes a little while to work out. But I mastered it.

RANTING (*taking hat off*). You got your head screwed on right. You go to the dog tracks in the evening?

CLERK. Not for me, Mr. Ranting.

RANTING. Horses?

CLERK. No horses, neither.

RANTING. You must spiel something. Poker, shemmy?

CLERK (*rising and moving behind his stool*). I'm developing myself, Mr. Ranting.

RANTING. Something new?

CLERK. The human frame has nine hundred seventy six individual muscles, each of whom can be developed up to peak power, give proper exercises and consideration.

RANTING. Nearly a thousand? So many?

CLERK. It has been proved by the best efficiency authorities that each of these muscular resources is vital to one. And what do we do?

You sit cramped—like this. The muscles get slack and useless. You stand like this. The muscles suffer.

RANTING. Sit and stand you can't avoid.

CLERK (*taking off his overalls*). Look at this, Mr. Ranting. (*Rolls up sleeve and demonstrates muscle.*)

RANTING. Marvellous. Like Kid Berg. You should be a boxer.

CLERK. Worse thing you can do for the muscles, boxing. Fatal to the muscle tone.

RANTING. So what can you do with all them muscles?

CLERK. So far, I still have four hundred and eighty nine muscles undeveloped.

RANTING. And then?

CLERK. I hope to stand as Mr. Universe.

RANTING. A meshuggus. Put back the coat.

CLERK (*restoring coat and moving* D.S.R.). When I get these pecs up I'll take my first competition.

RANTING. Local? (*Picks up* CLERK'S *notebook.*)

CLERK. Down at the Roxy.

RANTING. Maybe I'll come.

CLERK. You'll enjoy it, Mr. Ranting. The body beautiful.

RANTING. So I'll enjoy it. The whilst Mr. Universe, go shut the door. (*Pushes* CLERK *out* D.R. *and follows him.*)

SCENE 15

MORRY *and* FENDER *enter* D.L. *and move towards area* "B" *where the light now is. They come in arm in arm, singing and stumbling.* MORRY *carries an empty beer crate.*

MORRY. In your position, Fender, it's not professional to drink so much at once.

FENDER. You know I met Lennie?

MORRY. You were saying before. How is he doing?

FENDER. Very nice. They let him open a little stall outside the hotel, on the promenade. You can get any kind of herring from him.

MORRY (*puts crate down and stands on it*). I get in the window and give you a lift up. Just a minute. (*Gets down.*) See if you can walk through the wall.

FENDER (*crossing to* R. *of* MORRY, *pauses*). Don't talk silly, Morry.

MORRY. If you're a ghost you can walk through walls. And if you're not a ghost at least it's scientific experiment.

FENDER. It's true. I'll try. (*He tries.*) I feel silly. Get through the window, Morry. Just a minute. (*Takes key from pocket.*) A solution. I'll go round and open the door. (*Exit* D.R.)

MORRY (*gets on crate and tries to open window*). I can give myself a stricture with this. Shift, you—it don't budge. Get up.

FENDER (*off*). I done it. Come round. It's cold in here.

MORRY (*getting off crate and picking it up*). It would be nice if he walked through the wall, like I told him. (*Moving* R.) I even got to tell him how to be a ghost proper. (*Exit* D.R. *Blackout.*)

SCENE 16

Area "A". FENDER *enters* U.S.C. *with a torch and crosses* R. *to switch on imaginary light.*

FENDER. It's easy. You should try. I'll just switch on the light.

MORRY (*follows him in as the lights come on*). Right. Now, let's see. You remember where the coat is?

FENDER (*moving* U.S. *of stool*). Wait a minute. Trousers over there. Jackets here. (*Turns to audience.*) Would you believe it? I haven't been away five minutes and they shift the jackets.

MORRY (*moving to* U.S. *of coat rack*). Here are the coats. What about this? What a terrible cut. This one?

FENDER (*taking his old coat off and examining coat rack*). Not for me.

MORRY. The blue is nice.

FENDER. No.

MORRY. It's a silk lining. A good lining.

FENDER. For what?

MORRY. This?

FENDER. Too short. (*Takes out coat with sheepskin lining.*) Ah! Ah! This is different. This I'll take.

MORRY. It's a nice weight, Fender, (*Helping him on with it.*) but the workmanship. Not nice.

FENDER (*moving* D.S.C.). How many times do I have to tell you, Morry? It's not personal. Only I must have one of Ranting's coats. That's all. He owes me. (*On these lines* FENDER *becomes, it seems to us and to* MORRY, *less mobile, more like a dead man.*)

MORRY (*moving* D.S. *to* R. *of* FENDER). Terrible cold in here. So. Can you go?

FENDER. I can go.

MORRY. My work is better.

FENDER. Certainly your work is better.

MORRY. So now you're all right, heh?

FENDER. I feel all right.

MORRY. Fender, you know something. (*Hesitates.*) This brandy is good.

FENDER. So—thank you, Morry.

MORRY. So, Fender, you're going now? You'll go back to the hotel?

FENDER (*turning* U.S.). Where else have I got to go to?

MORRY. Fenderler—you should give to Lennie my best regards.

FENDER (*turning back to* MORRY). He's selling herrings like hot cakes, all day long. (*Moves* U.S.) He'll be pleased. A long life to you, Morry. Pray for me. (*His voice fades on this line and he has gone.*)

MORRY (*calls after him*). May you come to your place in peace, Fender. (*Putting his hat on to pray.*) Yiskadal, Veyiskaddish, . . .

The Hebrew Prayer for the dead is broken by barrel-organ music, off, as MORRY'S head sinks upon his chest. Slow CURTAIN as light fades.

THE END

Lightning Source UK Ltd.
Milton Keynes UK
UKOW06f0718260915

259315UK00001B/6/P